GLOUCESTER · CHELTENHAM

BISHOPS CLEEVE · QUEDGELEY · SHURDINGTON · UPTON ST. LEONARDS

V. S. P

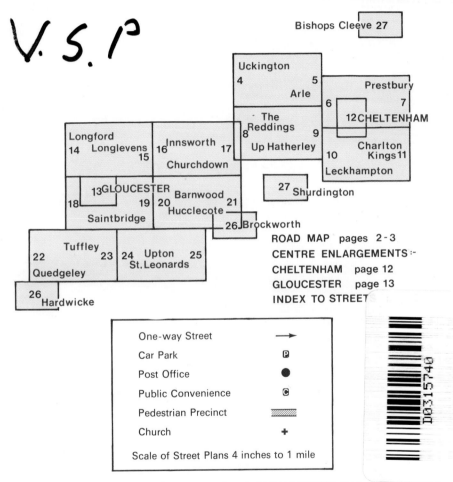

Bishops Cleeve 27

Uckington 4

Arle 5

Prestbury 7

6

12 CHELTENHAM

· The Reddings 8

Up Hatherley 9

Charlton Kings 11

10

Leckhampton

Longford 14

Longlevens 15

Innsworth 16 17

Churchdown

13 GLOUCESTER

19 20 Barnwood 21

Hucclecote

18

27 Shurdington

Saintbridge

26 Brockworth

Tuffley 22 23

24 Upton St. Leonards 25

Quedgeley

26 Hardwicke

ROAD MAP   pages   2 - 3

CENTRE ENLARGEMENTS :-

CHELTENHAM   page 12

GLOUCESTER   page 13

INDEX TO STREET

One-way Street	→
Car Park	℗
Post Office	●
Public Convenience	ⒸG
Pedestrian Precinct	▨
Church	+

Scale of Street Plans 4 inches to 1 mile

Street Plans prepared and published by ESTATE PUBLICATIONS, Bridewell House, Tenterden, Kent, and based upon the ORDNANCE SURVEY maps with the sanction of the Controller of H.M. Stationery Office.

All maps drawn by R. Griffiths and M. Stephens.

The publishers acknowledge the co-operation of Gloucester City Council, Cheltenham B.C., Tewkesbury B.C., & Stroud D.C. in the preparation of these maps.

ISBN 0 86084 348 3

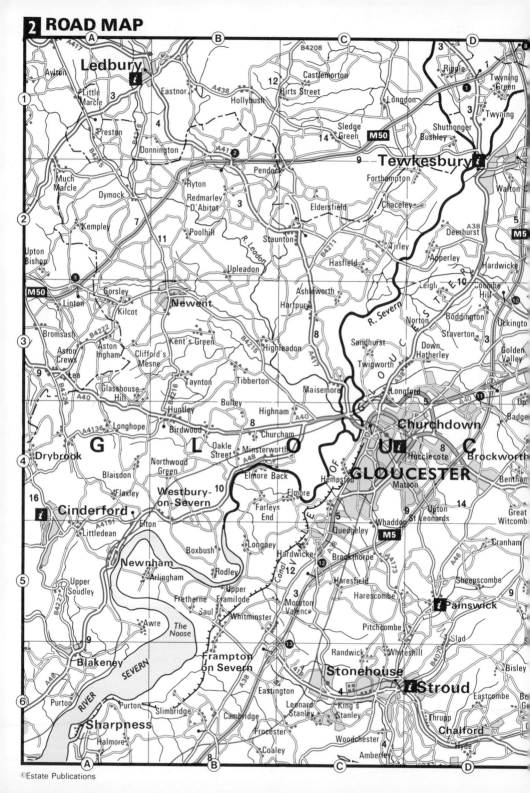

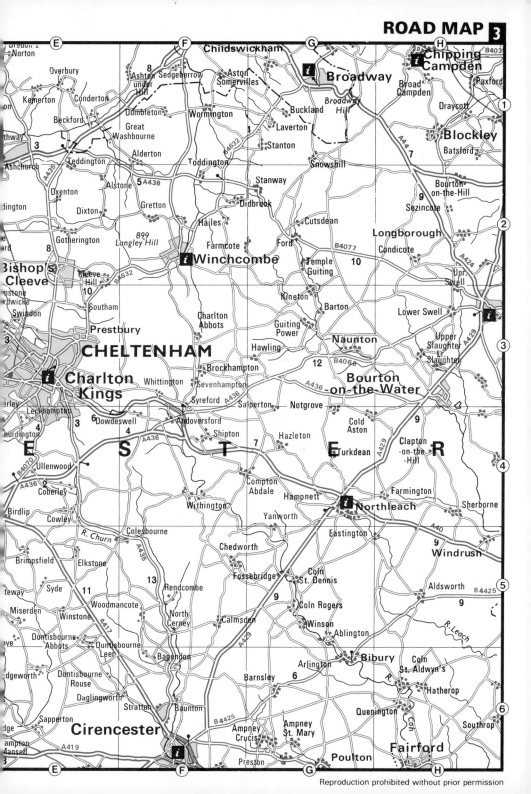

4 UCKINGTON

Sheldon Nurseries

A4019

TEWKESBURY

JUNCTION 10

WITHYBRIDGE GARDENS

WITHYBRIDGE LANE

ROAD

Manor Farm

Butlers Court

Subway

Boddington Coppice

Withy Bridge

River Chelt

Millhouse Farm

WITHYBRIDGE LANE

Uckington

Moat House

M5

Pilgrove Farm

Hayden Hill

OLD GLOUCESTER ROAD

P.H.

GLOUCESTER ROAD

HAYDEN LANE

Hayden Farm

WITHYBRIDGE ROAD

Hope Farm

Whitehall Farm

Hayden

HENLEY ROAD
STREET
HARTBURY CLOSE
SPRINGBANK
SOLWA
DUNS
ILLEY ROAD
NETTING TON CL
HARTBURY
SPRINGBANK DR
SPRINGBANK
HENLEY RD
ASTON GRO
SYCAMO
LABIRN CUM

Hayden Green

Water Pollution Control Centre

B4063

OLD GLOUCESTER ROAD

Home Farm

Swindon

The Orchard

Uckington Farm

Moat

TEWKESBURY

Swindon Hall

Manor Farm

Eng Works

Playing Field

DARK LANE

STANTONS DR

HULBERT

RIVELANDS

QUAT

GOOSE LANE

CHURCH ROAD

SMYTHE RD

MANOR CL

RUNNINGS ROAD

THE RUNNINGS

Wks

MACKENZIE WY

INDUSTRIAL ESTATE

MALMESBURY ROAD

HUNTSCOTE ROAD

KINGSVILLE ROAD

UPPERFIELD RD

KINGSDITCH

WYMANS LANE

Wks

CHOSEN VIEW

SWINDON ROAD

Swindon Farm

Engineering Works

Sainsburys

Club

Sports Ground

RIVER LEYS VIEND

P.H.

GLOUCESTER ROAD

River Chelt

Bar Bridge

HOMECROFT DRIVE

MANOR ROAD

RUTHERFORD

PATTERDALE

GLYN BRIDGE GDNS

CARTER

SHEP WK

GEORGE

RIVERVIEW ROAD

FRANK BROOKS CT

HOWELL

READINGS WAY

STRAND

Arle

Depot

Factory

Wks

ARLE INDUSTRIAL ESTATE

Eng Wks

TEWKESBURY

OLD

BRISTMILL

PILGROVE

GOUGH WAY

WILLIAM

BUSHEY

BARLEY CL

YATES

WY

THORN

NERGATE RD

WYNBROOK DR

HARVEST CARROLL

SPRING BANK GRO

CROFT

BLAKE CROFT

BEAUMONT DR

HESTERS

BEAUMONT

Playing Field

Playing Field

Schools

Old Peoples Home

VILLAGE ROAD

KINGSMEAD

HOWELL RD

WELCH ROAD

ISMAY RD

DILL AVENUE

LIPSON ROAD

HESTERS WAY

HOME

Play Field

Elec Schs

KINGSMEAD RD

DORMER RD

PRINCESS WAY

PENNSYLVANIA AVENUE

REDGROVE RD

KINGSMEAD CL

GREVIL RD

ELIZABETH AVENUE

BROCKLYN

CHELT WALK

CL

LEE

LEE

LEE

CHELT WALK

BROOKLYN GARDENS

BROOK RD

MOORS

ST PETER'S SQ

SAINT PET

ARNOLD ROAD

AVENUE

SLS

Rec Grd

Tewkesbury Bridge

TEWKESBURY ROAD A4019

RICHARDS

BRIDGE ST

Playing Field

Gasholder

Schools

CHELTENHAM IND PARK

ENTERPRIZE WAY

CENTRAL

Hesters Way

ASHLANDS ROAD

OLBURY RD

FALK LAND

WALK

GRAHAM

BARBRIDGE

ELIZABETH

HAWTHORN

BRAMLEY ROAD

RUSSET ROAD

TANNERS ROAD

ORCHARD AVENUE

BLENHEIM SQUARE

ORCHARD AVENUE

PRINCESS

DOWTY ROAD

ELLISON ROAD

KEYNSHAM RD

Health Centre

School

Playing Field

Club

Depot

WENT

STANLEY

HICKS BEECH

WINTERBOTHAM ROAD

Playing Field

School

Market

King Georges Field

Schools

Playing Field

BROOKLYN ROAD

BEDFORD

CLEVEDON SQUARE

CORNWALL AV

DEVON AV

MERRI VILLE GDNS

NETHER WOOD GARDENS

ARLE DRIVE

ARLE

ARLE GARDENS

AVE CORNWALL

BRYANSTON

Arle Road Bridge

Sports Ground

ARLE AV

STIRLING CL

CENTRAL

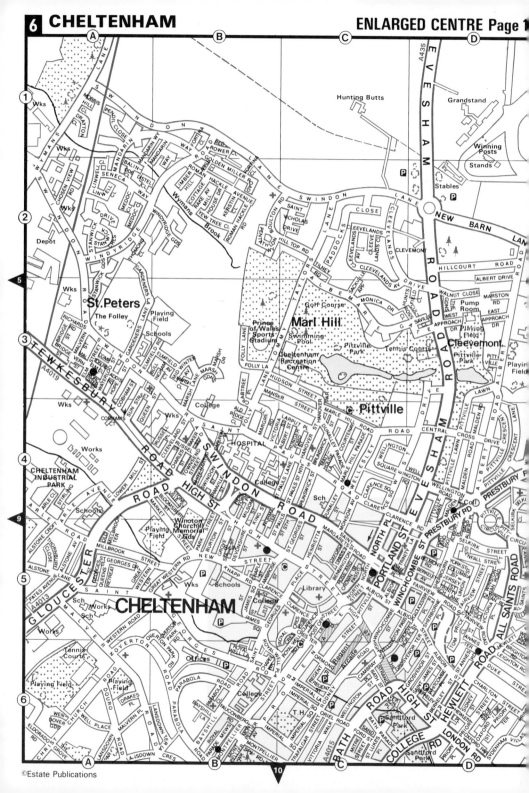

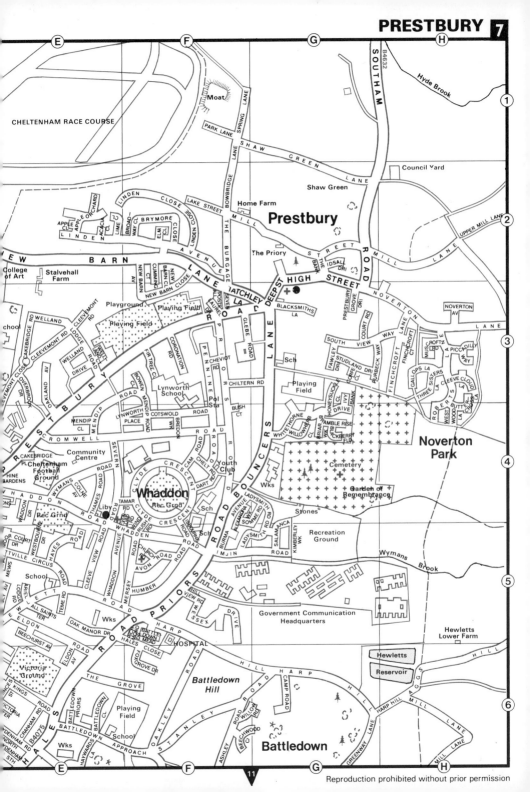

E F G H

B4632

Hyde Brook

SOUTHAM

CHELTENHAM RACE COURSE

1

Moat

Council Yard

PARK LANE
SPRING LANE
SHAW GREEN LANE
Shaw Green

LAKE STREET
BOWBRIDGE LANE

Home Farm

Prestbury

2

UPPER MILL LANE
MILL ROAD

LINDEN CLOSE
BROAD WAY CL
BRYMORE CL
ELM CL
LINDEN CLOSE CLOSE
CUMMING ST
APPLE ORCHARD
APPLE CL
ACACIA CL
LIME CL
LINDEN

The Priory

STREET
THE BANK
IDSALL DRI

NEW BARN

NEW BARN CL
NEW BARN AV

College of Art

Stalvehall Farm

AVENUE
LANE

HATCHLEY LA
DEEP ST
HIGH STREET

POSTER
LAUREL
GLEBE

Blacksmiths LA

PRESTBURY GROVE
COURT RD
DRI
NOVERTON

NOVERTON AV

LANE 3

School

CLEEVEMONT RD
CLEEVEMONT
RD
WELLAND
CAKEBRIDGE RD
WELLAND RD
LODGE RD

OAKLAND AV
WOODBRIDGE
LEVEMONT CLOSE
DRI

FIR TREE CL
CORONATION RD
PENNINE RD
CHEVIOT RD
CHILTERN RD

GLEBE ROAD

BUSH CT

Playground
Playing Field
Playing Field

Lynworth School

Pol Sta

SOUTH VIEW
Sch

FAWLEY DRI
STUDLAND DRI
PURBECK WAY
WAY
FINCHCROFT
FINCHCROFT CT
ROBERTS LA
WEST
MUS
CROFT
GALLOPS LA
THREE SISTERS
CLEEVE CLOUD
WOODBUTTS LA
PICCADILLY WAY

LANE 3

Playing Field

NEW BARN LANE

PRESTBURY ROAD

CROMWELL
MENDIP
SEVERN
COLNE RD
THAMES ROAD
CLYDE CRESCENT
CAM
CHELT
DART
WYMANS ROAD

MENDIP CL
LYNWORTH PLACE
COTSWOLD WR
BREDON RD

Lynworth Road

Community Centre

Cheltenham Football Ground

CAKEBRIDGE PL

RHINE GARDENS

WHADDON RD

Whaddon

Rec Grnd

Liby

TAMAR RD
RUSH RD
WHADDON AVENUE
CLEEVE VIEW RD

ROAD BOUNCERS LANE

Youth Club

Sch
Sch
Sch

LADYSMITH
AVENUE
BURMA RD
ALEXANDER
SOMME RD
LADYSMITH RD
SALAMANCA RD
KIMBERLEY WK

WHITETHORNE
WILLOW
BRIAR
HONEYSUCKLE
IVY
RISE
AMBLE RISE
BLACKBERRY CL

Sch

Playing Field

Wks

Cemetery

Noverton Park

4

Garden of Remembrance

Stones

Recreation Ground

Wymans Brook

5

School

BRIERLY
ARIEL
ALL SAINTS TER
COURT MEWS
OTTVILLE CIRCUS

W
ELDON RD
TEME RD
W

IMJIN ROAD
HARP VIEW RD
WESSEX DRIVE

Government Communication Headquarters

Hewletts Lower Farm

Wks

OAK MANOR DR

BATTLEDOWN
BATTLEDOWN MEAD
HALES CLOSE
GROVE DR

HOSPITAL

HARP ROAD
HILL ROAD
HARP ROAD
CAMP ROAD

Hewletts

Reservoir

HILL

Victoria Ground

KINGS
VICTORIA RD
PRINCES
NORTH UP

ELDON AV
BATTLEDOWN PRIORS
BATTLEDOWN CL

THE GROVE

Battledown Hill

ROAD
WILLOW
BEECHWOOD

HARP HILL
MILL LANE

6

B4075

BATTLEDOWN APPROACH
HAYWARDS LA
School
Wks

OAKLEY RD
STANLEY RD
ASHLEY RD
BEECHURST AV

HILL
GREENWAY LANE
MILL LANE

Battledown

HALES ROAD
PRIORS ROAD

E F G H

Reproduction prohibited without prior permission

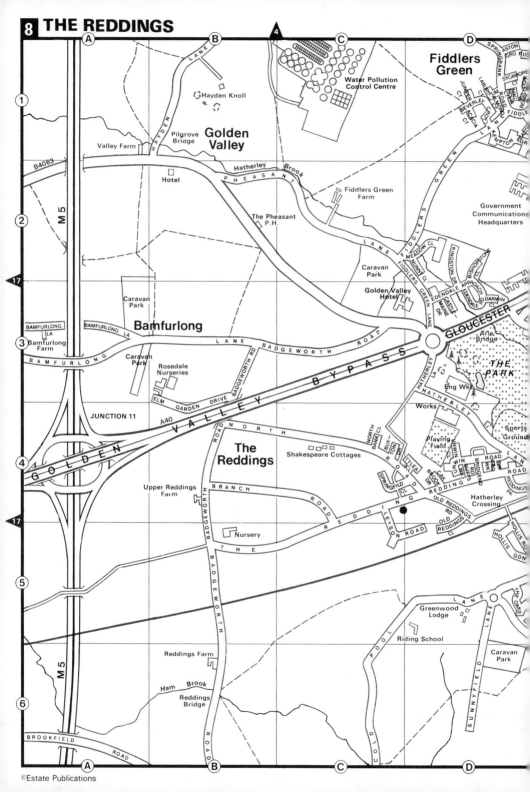

Fiddlers Green

Water Pollution Control Centre

Hayden Knoll

Pilgrove Bridge

Golden Valley

Valley Farm

B4063

Hotel

Hatherley Brook

Fiddlers Green Farm

The Pheasant P.H.

Government Communications Headquarters

M 5

Caravan Park

Caravan Park

Golden Valley Hotel

GLOUCESTER

Arle Bridge

Bamfurlong

BAMFURLONG LA

Bamfurlong Farm

BADGEWORTH ROAD

LANE

THE PARK

Eng Wks

BAMFURLONG LA

Caravan Park

Rosedale Nurseries

ELM GARDEN DRIVE

Works

A40

JUNCTION 11

GOLDEN VALLEY BYPASS

HATHERLEY LA

HATHERLEY LANE

Sports Ground

ROAD NORTH

Shakespeare Cottages

NORTH BANK CL

Playing Field

The Reddings

SPRINGFILD CL

REDDING

Hatherley Crossing

OLD REDDINGS RD

OLD REDDINGS CL

Upper Reddings Farm

BADGEWORTH

BRANCH ROAD

THE REDDING LEVSON ROAD

HOLLIS RD

HOLLIS GDN

Nursery

THE BADGEWORTH ROAD

Greenwood Lodge

THE OAKS

Reddings Farm

Riding School

Caravan Park

SUNNYFIELD LANE

Ham Brook

Reddings Bridge

M 5

BROOKFIELD ROAD

©Estate Publications

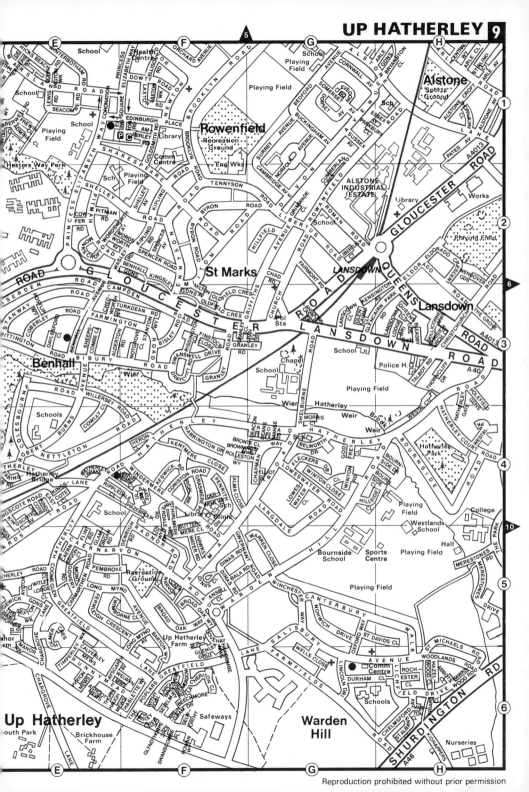

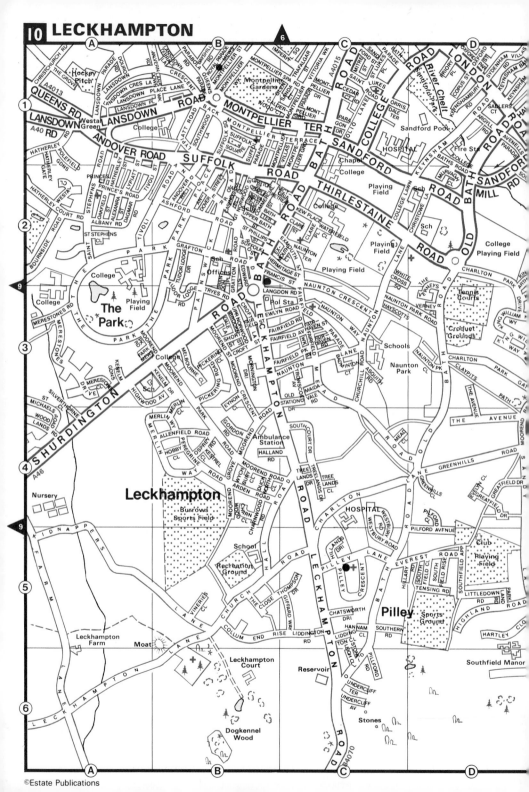

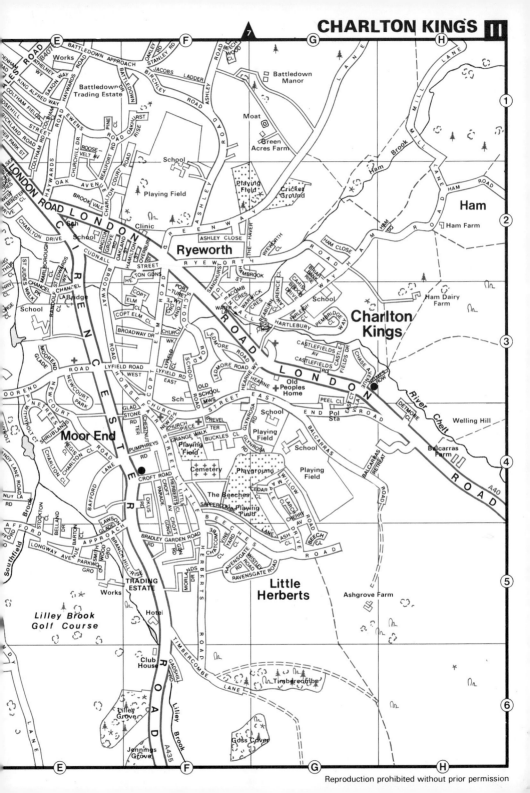

7

E F G H

1

2

3

4

5

6

Ham

Charlton Kings

Ryeworth

Moor End

Little Herberts

Lilley Brook Golf Course

Battledown Trading Estate

Battledown Manor

Green Acres Farm

Cricket Ground

Playing Field

Ham Farm

Ham Dairy Farm

Welling Hill

Balcarras Farm

Old Peoples Home

Cemetery

Playground

The Beeches

Ashgrove Farm

Club House

Lilley Grove

Jennings Grove

Goss Cover

Timbercombe

River Chelt

A40 ROAD

LONDON ROAD

CIRENCESTER ROAD

HORSEFAIR STREET

CHURCH STREET

TIMBERCOMBE ROAD

A435 Lilley Brook ROAD

Works

Hotel

TRADING ESTATE

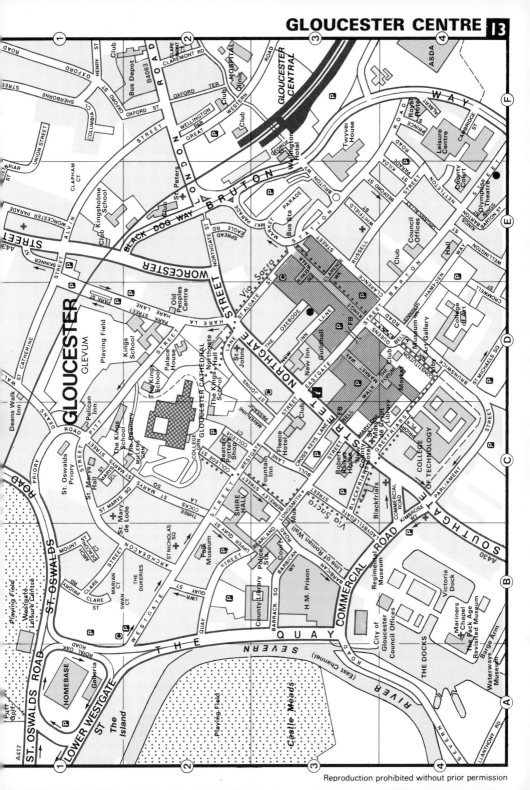

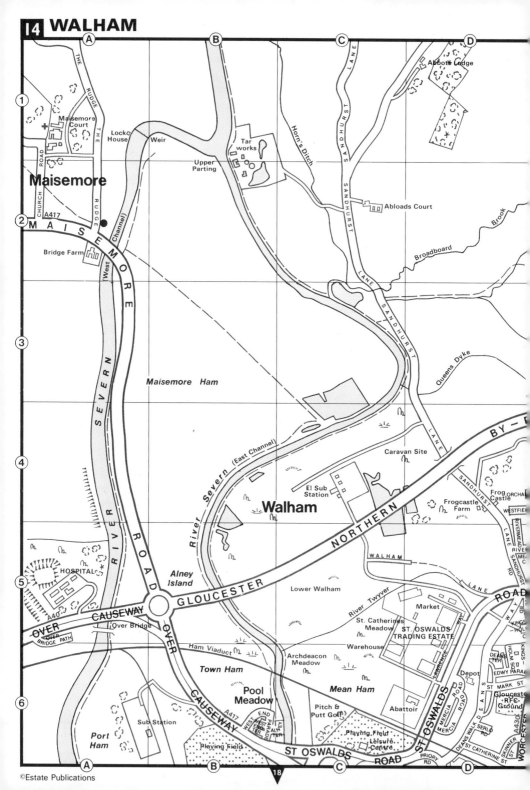

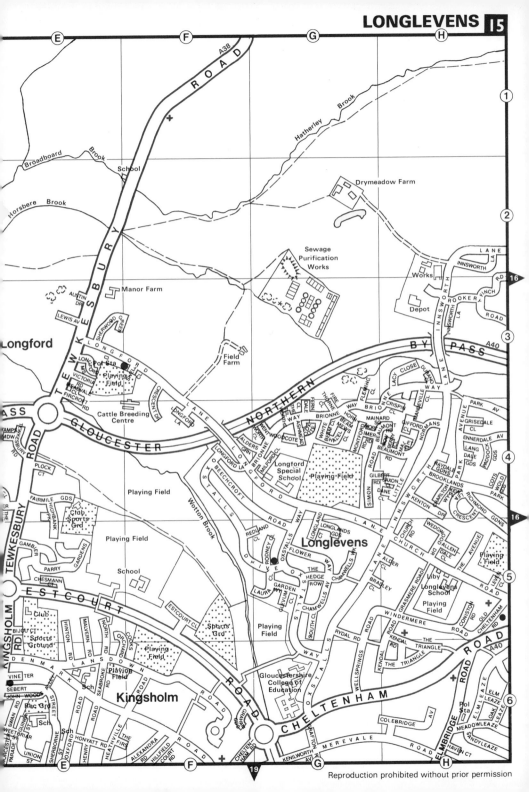

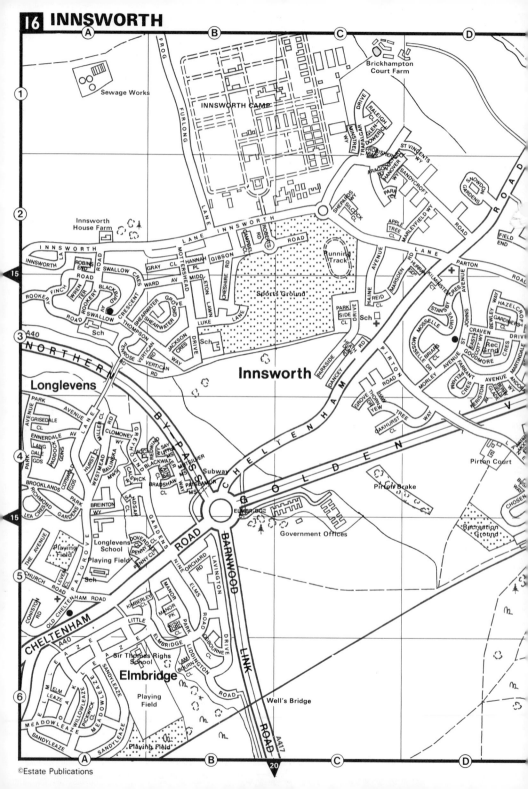

Sewage Works

INNSWORTH CAMP

Brickhampton
Court Farm

1

Innsworth House Farm

Running Track

Innsworth

15

FROG
FURLONG
LANE

INNSWORTH LANE

Sports Ground

2

RALEIGH
MINSTREL WY
TRAFALGAR
GLEN DR
DOWER CL
FISHER MWS
DRAGONFLY WY
FANGFOSS WY
SANDYCROFT
ST VINCENT'S
PARK CL
APPLE TREE CL
MARLEYFIELD WY
NOWD GARDENS
PARTON LANE
FIELD END

INNSWORTH LA
ROBINS END
WREN TER
FINCH
ROOKERY
ROOKERY
BLACKSMITH
SWALLOW CRES
SWALLOW
GRAY CL
HANNAH PL
MORSHEAD
WARD AV
MIDDLETON LAWN
GIBSON
CAMPBELL RD
CHESHIRE RD
ROBERTS RD
INNSWORTH ROAD
HAINE
HURST CL
MARSDEN RD
KILMINSTER CRES
STANSBY DRIVE
SCOTT W
PARTON
AVENUE
ROAD

Longlevens

3

A40
NORTHERN
THOMPSON
SHEARWATER
SHEARWATER
CRESCENT
JACKSON CRES
ROSE
VERTICAN
VERTICAN RD
LUKE LANE
GROVE
BY-PASS
Sch
Sch
PARK SIDE CL
PARKSIDE RD
DANCEY RD
GROVE
HAINE
REID CL
DRIVE
PIRTON ROAD
MOSSELLE DRIVE
MOSSELLE
BRIARS CL
ST JOHNS
CRAVEN CRES
EAST W
GOODMORE
MORLEY AVENUE
AVENUE
FARRANT CRES
HERISTON
GOODMORE CRES
HAZELCROFT
GARDINERS CL
MARTINDALE
DRIVE
ANCHOR WY

15

4

PARK
AVENUE
GRISEDALE CL
ENNERDALE
LANG DALE GDS
PADDOCK GDS
BROOKLANDS
RICHMOND GARDENS
LEA CRES
COTSWOLD GDS
HURST RD
WESTMEAD
BALLINDRA MWS
MILLER CL
CLOMONEY WY
GREYHOUND RD
JACKA
SAVERY CL
REDWIND
BLACKWATER
CL
PICK
SILVER CL
LITTLE MS
BRADSHAW
PATESMUIR
CL
MS
BREINTON WY
LANSDALE
DOVER CL
GREENWAY
PAYGROVE
Longlevens School
Playing Field
Playing Field
Sch
GARDENS
PENNY CL
ELMBRIDGE ROAD
BARNWOOD ROAD
Subway
ELMBRIDGE
Government Offices
CHELTENHAM
GOLDEN
Pirton Court
Pirton Brake
Recreation Ground
CHOSEN
CHOSEN WY

5

CHURCH
CLEVEL
Sch
CONISTON RD
OLD CHELTENHAM ROAD
KIMBERLEY CL
MANOR RD
MANOR PK
LITTLE
ELMBRIDGE
WISH
NINE ORCHARD RD
ELMS
LAVINGTON
PARK ROAD
OSBOURNE DRIVE
LIDDINGTON RD
BURNINGTON CL
Playing Field
CHELTENHAM
A40
Sir Thomas Righs School
Elmbridge
LINK
Well's Bridge
ROAD
A417

6

M ELM LEAZE
WILLOWLEAZE
PICKWICK
MEADOWLEAZE
SANDYLEAZE
MEADOWLEAZE
SANDYLEAZE
LEAZE
Playing Field
Playing Field

20

GLOUCESTER & CHELTENHAM (STAVERTON) AIRPORT

Bamfurlong Farm

BAMFURLONG

LA

LANE

JUNCTION 11

B4063 ROAD

CHELTENHAM

Parton Farm

Evergreen Farm

Parton Manor

BITTERMILK LANE

SPRINGWELL

WINSLOW

GARDENS

PARTON

GOLDEN VALE

GOLDEN

Sch

QUINTON

BY-PASS

A40

Norman's

Brook

Home Farm

M5

ROAD

Community Centre

Parton Court

Churchdown

Playing Field

School

PARTON ROAD

SUMMER LAND

PARTON AVENUE

COCHRAN

PARTON DR

STATION CL

MELVILLE RD

WINSTON

BADER

SWALE

BARNES WAY

HARRIS CL

BOWDLING WAY

TRUEMAN

CAVENDISH

Sports Ground

School

BROOKFIELD LANE

PARTON ROAD

SANDFIELD PLOCKS

SANDFIELD ROAD

FAR SANDFIELD

Playing Field

Police Station

Sch

THE AVENUE

THE PIECE

Liby

THE MANOR

CHURCH

HOW CROFT

STATION ROAD

CORDINGLEY CL

CORDINGLEY LANE

LANE

VICARAGE

Rec Grd

CHAPEL

P

DRIVE

DANIELS WY

THE PLOCKS

AVENUE

KILBOURNE CRES

ALBEMARLE

BLACKSMITH LA

ORCHARD DR

BROOKFIELD ROAD

ORCHARD

KINGSCOTE

CROFT CL

HAY LANE

PAYNES PITCH

OLDBURY

ORCHARD CL

DUNSTANS

ODBURY

CRANHAM LA

ANN HATHAWAY DR

ROAD

Whitehouse Farm

GREEN LA

DREWS COURT

CRIFTYCRAFT LANE

GREEN LANE

BARROW HILL

HUCCLECOTE RD

Tinkers Hill

The Green

BROCKWORTH

ROAD

Woodfield Farm

✠ *Churchdown Hill*

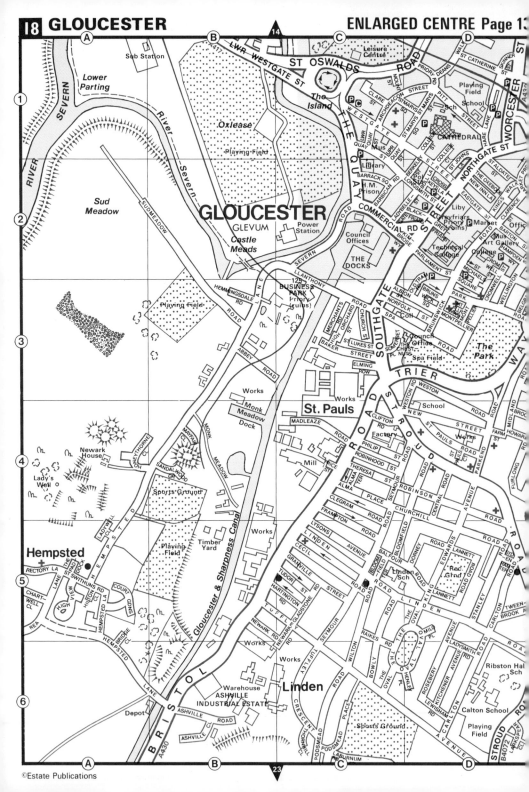

GLOUCESTER

GLEVUM

Hempsted

St. Pauls

Linden

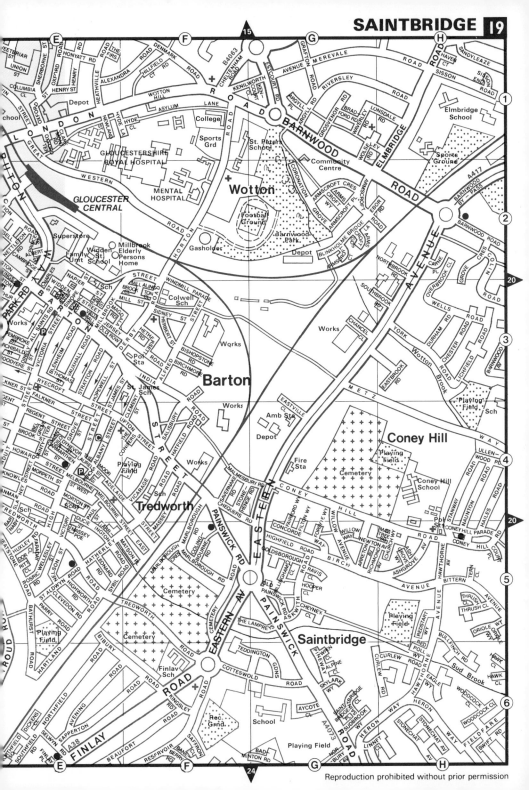

Grid references: E F G H along top and bottom; 1 2 3 4 5 6 along right edge.

Reservoir

The Brake

Reservoir

Soldiers Walk

Woodlands Farm

Churchdown Hill

The Coombs

Covered Reservoir

Pressmead Farm

BROCKWORTH ROAD

M5

LANE HUCCLECOTE

Noake Court Farm

THE NOAKE

CHURCHDOWN

Dean Farm

Roman Villa (site of)

Hucclecote School

Playing Field

BY PASS

Horsbere Brook

Brockworth Court

Brockworth

Playing Field

Club

Sports Ground

GLOUCESTER TRADING ESTATE

AIRFIELD

I.C.I. Works

ERMIN

SUSSEX GARDENS

COLERNE DRIVE

SUSSEX GARDENS

HUCCLECOTE ROAD

HAM CT

FRONT AV

CEDAR ROAD

MAPLE DR

ROWAN

PARK GARDENS

OAK

ELM DR

PRINCE ALBERT CT

WESTFIELD AV

ASTOR CL

WESTFIELD LA

GOLF CLUB

HILLVIEW AV

Pol Sta

BOVERTON ROAD

ERMIN

PARK DRIVE

BOVERTON DRIVE

ST ANNES CL

FAIRHAVEN DR

ANSDELL DR

AVENUE

BOVERTON

BOVERTON AVENUE

RIDGEMOUNT CL

SAYERS CRES

VICARAGE CT

MOORFIELD COURT

Liby

ROAD

HICKLEY GDS

HURCOMBE WAY

TANNERS WAY

Sports Ground

MILL LANE

Sch

Mill Farm

Playing Field

TAMAR RD

CLYDE ROAD

TRENT RD

LEADON CL

LEA ROAD

MED WAY

ROAD

MERSEY WAY

DERWENT RD

ROAD

STREET

STREET

GREEN

GREEN BK

SEABROOK RD

GREEN WAY

ABBOTSWOOD ROAD

A417

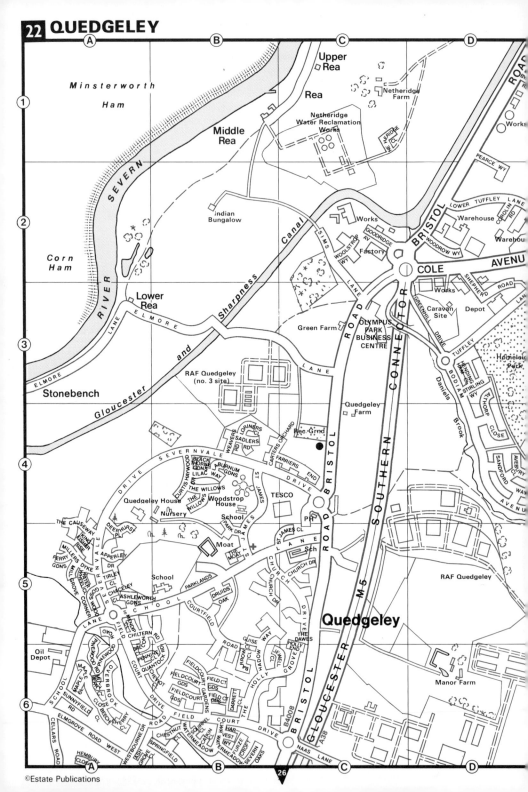

©Estate Publications

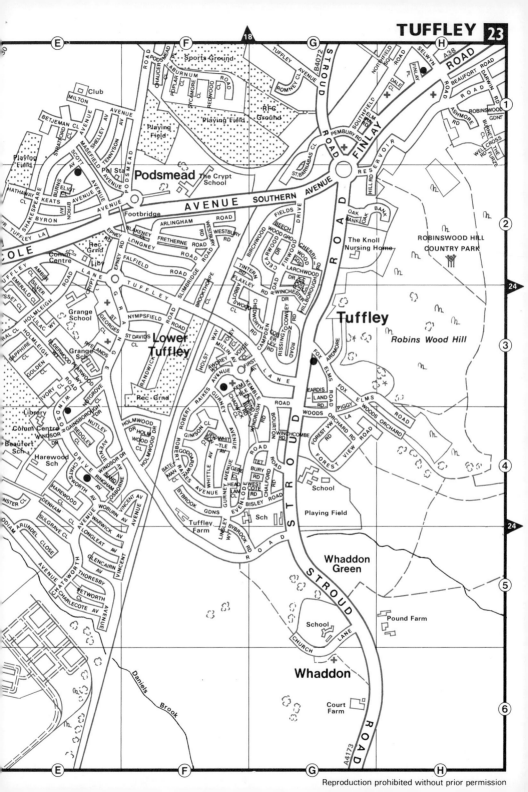

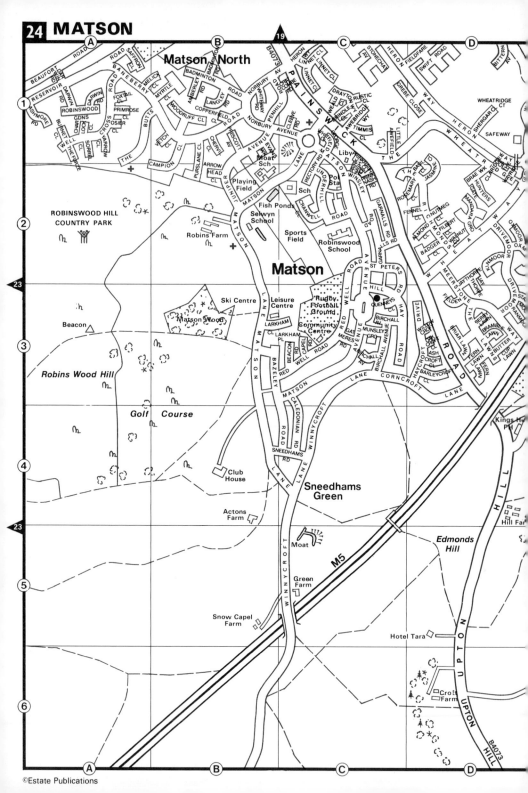

Matson North

Matson

Sneedhams Green

Edmonds Hill

ROBINSWOOD HILL COUNTRY PARK

Robins Wood Hill

Golf Course

Beacon

Matson Wood

Ski Centre

Leisure Centre

Community Centre

Rugby Football Ground

Club House

Actons Farm

Moat

Green Farm

Snow Capel Farm

Hotel Tara

Croft Farm

Hill Farm

Kings Hd Ph

Wheatridge Ct

Safeway

Robins Farm

Robinswood School

Selwyn School

Sports Field

Fish Ponds

Playing Field

Moat Sch

Sch

Pol Sta

M5

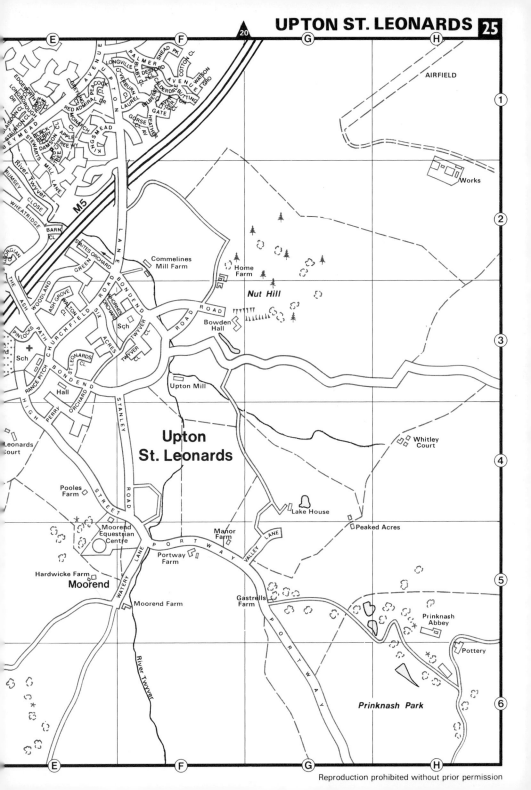

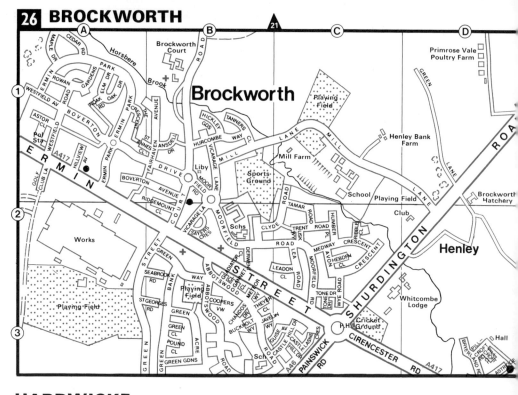

©Estate Publications

HARDWICKE

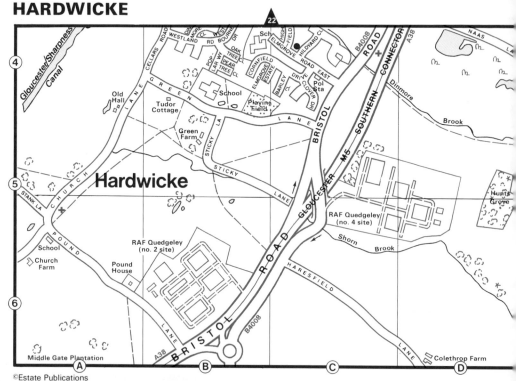

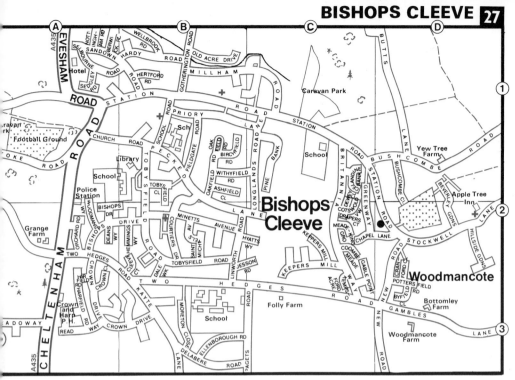

Bishops Cleeve

Evesham Road · A435 · Hotel · Selbourne Road · Sandown Road · Hertford Rd · Nott Ham Rd · Berw Ex Rc · Wellbrook Rd · Hardy Road · Gotherington Road · Old Acre Drive · Millham Road · Station Road · Caravan Park · Butts · Yew Tree Farm · Bushcombe Lane · Station Road · Apple Tree Inn · Beverley Gdns · Hillside Gdns · Stockwell · Woodmancote · Potters Field · Bottomley Farm · Gambles Lane · Woodmancote Farm

Football Ground · Cheltenham Road · Church Road · Library · School · Police Station · Grange Farm · Bishops Dr · Deans Wy · Two Hedges · Crown Cl · Harfield Rd · Crown Rd · Kayte · Crown Drive · Way · Read · Crownland Harp P.H. · Priory Road · Sch · Pecked Lane · Fieldgate Road · Oak Field Rd · Birch Field · Withyfield Rd · Ashfield Cl · Oakfield Rd · Minetts Av · Saint Mich · Courtiers Dr · Cummings Rd · Dale Rd · Tobysfield Road · Toby Field Cl · Tobysfield · Longlands Road · Pine Bank · Avenue · Linworth Rd · Hyatts Wy · Jesson Rd · Moreton Close · Ellenborough Rd · Delabere Road · Pagets · Folly Farm · School · Two Hedges Road

Bishops Cleeve

Keepers Mill · Chapel Lane · Britannia Road · Bushcombe Cl · Greenway Road · Station Road · Cotswold Vw · Delevere Rd · Drapers Ct · Mead Gro · Commercial Mead · Gable Porn · Cran Ford Cl · New Road · Byf Cl

Woodmancote

SHURDINGTON

Road · A46 · Ham Brook · Shurdington Bridge · Playing Field · Leckhampton Lane · Bickford House · Gables Farm · nfield Farm · Sch · Church Farm · School Lane · Blenheim · Orchard · Vicarage · Church · Cowls Mead · Com Cent · Lawn Cres · Dutch Farm · Home Farm · Laurence Cl · Bishop Road · Harrison Road · Wilson Rd · Gardens · Sinclair Rd · Yarnolds · Lambert Ter · Lambert Avenue · Lambert Cl · Lambert Dr · Green Way · Lamb Cl · School · Shurdington · Farm La · Yarnolds · Shurdington House Stables · Shurdington Grove · Shurdington Lane · A46 · Greenway Lane · Cowley Farm · Ridgeworth

Shurdington

INDEX TO STREETS

Grange Walk 11 F4
Granley Clo 9 F3
Granley Dri 9 G3
Granley Rd 9 F3
Granville St 6 B4
Grasmere Rd 9 F4
Gratton Rd 10 B2
Gratton St 10 B2
Great Norwood St 10 B2
Great Western Rd 6 A5
Great Western Ter 6 A5
Greatfield Dri 10 D4
Greatfield La 9 F6
Greenhills Clo 10 D4
Greenhills Rd 10 D4
Greenway La 11 F2
Grevil Rd 5 G5
Griffiths Av 9 G3
Grimwade Clo 9 G2
Gristmill Clo 5 E4
Grosvenor Place St 12 D3
Grosvenor St 12 D4
Grosvenor Ter 12 D3
Grove St 12 A1
Groveland 11 F3
Gwernant Rd 9 F5

Hales Clo 7 E5
Hales Rd 7 E6
Hall Rd 10 B5
Halland Rd 10 B4
Hallmead Clo 5 E4
Ham Clo 11 G2
Ham Rd 11 G2
Ham Sq 11 H2
Hambrook St 11 F2
Hamilton St 11 F2
Hampton Clo 9 H6
Hannam Clo 10 C5
Hanover Par 6 C4
Hanover St 6 C4
Harp Hill 7 F5
Harrington Dri 9 F4
Harry Yates Way 5 E4
Hartbury Clo 4 D6
Hartlebury Way 11 G3
Hartley Clo 10 D5
Harvest Gro 5 E4
Haslette Way 9 F6
Hatherley Brake 9 E4
Hatherley Court Rd 9 H4
Hatherley Gate 9 H4
Hatherley La 8 D3
Hatherley Rd 9 E5
Hatherley St 10 A2
Hawcombe Mews 9 F6
Hawkswater Rd 9 F5
Hawkswood Rd 9 H6
Hawthorn Rd 5 F6
Hayden La 4 B5
Hayes Rd 7 E5
Hayscotts 10 C3
Haywards Rd 11 E2
Hazebrouk Clo 9 F4
Hazelwood Clo 9 H6
Hazle Dean Rd 4 D4
Hazlitt Croft 5 E5
Hearne Clo 11 G3
Hearne Way 11 F3
Helens Clo 5 E5
Henley Rd 4 D6
Henrietta St 12 B2
Hereford Pl 6 B4
Hermitage St 10 B2
Heron Clo 9 F4
Hesters Way La 5 E5
Hesters Way Rd 5 E6
Hetton Gdns 11 F2
Hewlett Pl 6 D6
Hewlett Rd 6 D6
Hicks Beach Rd 5 E6
High St, Cheltenham 12 A1
High St, Prestbury 7 G2
Highland Rd 10 D5
Highwood Av 10 A3
Hill Top Rd 6 C2
Hill View Rd 7 F5
Hillands Dri 10 C5
Hillary Rd 10 C5
Hillcourt Rd 6 D2
Hillfield 9 G2
Hillside Clo 9 G4
Hine Gdns 7 E4
Hobby Clo 10 B4
Hollis Gdns 8 D5
Hollis Rd 8 D5
Home Clo 5 F5
Homecroft Dri 5 E3
Honeybourne Dri 5 E4
Honeysuckle Clo 7 G4
Hope St 6 A3
Horsefair St 11 E3
Howell Rd 5 F4
Hudson St 6 B3
Hulbert Clo 5 H2
Humber Rd 7 F5
Hungerford St 6 C4
Huntscote Rd 5 H3
Huntsfield Clo 6 D3

Idsall Dri 7 G2

Imjin Rd 7 F5
Imperial Circus 12 C3
Imperial La 12 B4
Imperial Sq 12 B4
INDUSTRIAL ESTATES:
Alstone Ind Est 9 G2
Arle Ind Est 5 H4
Battledown
Trading Est 11 E1
Cheltenham Ind Pk 5 H6
Isbourne Rd 7 F5
Ismay Rd 5 F5
Ivy Bank 7 G3

Jacobs Ladder 11 F1
Jersey Av 7 E5
Jersey St 6 D5
Joyner Rd 5 G4
Juniper Ct 8 D1

Kempton Gro 8 D1
Kenelm Dri 10 B3
Kenelm Gdns 10 A3
Kensington Av 9 H3
Kentmere Clo 9 F4
Kerstin Clo 6 B2
Kestrel Clo 10 B4
Keswick Rd 9 F4
Kew Pl 10 C2
Keynsham Bank 10 D1
Keynsham Rd 10 D2
Keynsham St 10 D1
Keynshambury Rd 10 D1
Kidnappers La 10 A5
Kimberley Walk 7 G5
King Alfred Way 11 E1
King Arthur Clo 11 E2
King George Clo 10 D3
King Henry Clo 10 D3
King St 12 A1
King William Way 10 D3
Kings Rd 7 E6
Kingscote Av 9 E4
Kingscote Clo 9 E4
Kingscote Cres 9 E4
Kingscote Road East 9 E4
Kingscote Road West 9 E5
Kingsditch La 5 H4
Kingsley Gdns 9 F2
Kingsmead Av 5 F5
Kingsmead Clo 5 G5
Kingsmead Rd 5 G5
Kingston Dri 8 D2
Kingsville Rd 5 H4
Kipling Rd 9 F2
Knapp La 12 A2
Knapp Rd 12 A2
Knightsbridge Cres 11 E2

Laburnum Ct 8 D1
Ladysmith Rd 7 G4
Lake St 7 F2
Langdale Rd 9 G4
Langdon Rd 10 B3
Langton Grove Rd 11 E2
Lansdown Castle Dri 9 G3
Lansdown Clo 9 G3
Lansdown Cres 10 A1
Lansdown Crescent La 10 A1
Lansdown Lodge Dri 9 H3
Lansdown Par 10 A1
Lansdown Pl 10 A1
Lansdown Place La 10 A1
Lansdown Rd 9 G3
Lansdown Terrace La 6 B6
Lansdown Walk 10 A1
Larch Clo 11 G4
Larchmere Gro 9 F6
Larput Pl 6 C4
Laurel Dri 7 F3
Lawrence Clo 11 G3
Lawson Glade 11 E4
Laxton Rd 9 F1
Laxton Walk 9 F1
Lechmere Rd 5 F6
Leckhampton La 10 A6
Leckhampton Rd 10 B3
Ledmore Rd 11 F3
Lee Clo 5 G5
Leighton Rd 6 D6
Lenster Clo 4 D5
Lewis Rd 9 E1
Leyson Rd 8 C4
Libertus Ct 9 G2
Libertus Rd 9 G2
Lichfield Dri 9 H6
Liddington Clo 10 C5
Liddington Rd 10 C5
Limber Hill 6 B2
Lime Clo 7 E2
Lincoln Dri 9 G6
Linden Av 7 E2
Linden Clo 7 F2
Linwell Clo 6 A2
Lipson Rd 5 F5
Little Bayshill Ter 12 A3
Little Herberts Clo 11 F4
Little Herberts Rd 11 F4
Littledown Rd 10 D5
Liverpool Pl 12 D3
London Rd 11 E2
Long Mynd Av 9 E5

Longway Av 11 E5
Lower Mill St 6 A4
Loweswater Clo 9 G4
Loweswater Rd 9 G4
Lyfield Clo 11 F3
Lyfield Road East 11 F3
Lyfield Road West 11 E3
Lygon Walk 5 G5
Lynworth Pl 7 F4
Lypiatt Rd 10 B1
Lypiatt St 10 A2

Mackenzie Way 5 G3
Magnolia Ct 8 D1
Maidavale Rd 10 C3
Malden Rd 6 D4
Malmesbury Rd 5 G4
Malthouse La 6 C4
Malvern Pl 6 A6
Malvern Rd 6 A5
Malvern St 6 A3
Mandarin Way 6 A1
Manor Clo 5 H2
Manor Rd 5 G4
Manse Gdns 9 G4
Manser St 6 B3
Maple Dri 11 G4
Margrett Rd 6 B3
Market St 6 A4
Marle Hill Par 6 C4
Marle Hill Rd 6 C4
Marsh Clo 6 B3
Marsh Dri 6 B3
Marsh Gdns 6 B3
Marsh La 6 B3
Marsland Rd 9 E1
Marston Rd 6 D3
Maythorn Dri 5 E4
Mead Clo 10 C4
Mead Rd 10 C3
Meadow Clo 8 D2
Meadow La 9 F6
Medoc Clo 6 A2
Melbourne Clo 10 B3
Mendip Clo 7 E4
Mendip Rd 7 E4
Merestones Clo 10 A3
Merestones Dri 10 A3
Merestones Rd 10 A3
Merlin Way 10 A4
Merriville Gdns 5 G6
Merriville Rd 5 G6
Mersey Rd 7 F5
Midwinter Av 6 B3
Mill House Dri 6 B2
Mill La 11 H2
Mill St 7 F2
Millbrook St 6 A5
Milsom St 6 B4
Milton Av 9 F3
Milton Rd 9 F2
Miserden Rd 9 E3
Mitre St 12 C5
Monica Dri 6 C3
Monkscroft 9 E2
Monson Av 12 C1
Montgomery Rd 9 E5
Montpellier Av 12 A5
Montpellier Dri 12 B6
Montpellier Gro 12 B6
Montpellier Par 12 B6
Montpellier Spa Rd 12 A5
Montpellier St 12 A5
Montpellier Ter 12 A6
Montpellier Villas 10 B1
Montpellier Walk 12 A5
Moor Court Dri 7 E5
Moorend Cres 10 B3
Moorend Glade 11 E3
Moorend Gro 10 B4
Moorend Park Rd 10 B3
Moorend Rd,
Leckhampton 10 B4
Moorend Rd, Moor End 11 E3
Moorend St 10 B3
Moors Av 5 H5
Morlands Dri 11 F5
Mornington Dri 10 B3
Morris Ct 9 G4
Morris Hill Clo 6 A1
Mulberry Ct 8 D1
Murvagh Clo 10 D2
Muscroft Rd 7 H3

Naunton Cres 10 C2
Naunton La 10 C3
Naunton Park Clo 10 D3
Naunton Park Rd 10 C3
Naunton Ter 10 C2
Naunton Way 10 C3
Nelmes Row 11 G3
Netherwood Gdns 5 G6
Nettleton Rd 9 E4
New Barn Av 7 F2
New Barn Clo 7 F2
New Barn La 6 D2
New St, Cheltenham 12 A2
New St, Moor End 11 F4
Newcourt Pk 11 E3
Newcourt Rd 11 E3
Newton Rd 5 F6
Norfolk Av 9 G2

Normal Ter 12 B1
North Hall Mew 7 E5
North Pl 12 C2
North Rd 8 B4
North St 12 C2
Northbank Clo 8 C4
Northfield Passage 12 C1
Northfield Ter 12 C1
Norwich Dri 9 G5
Notgrove Clo 9 F3
Noverton Av 7 H3
Noverton La 7 G3
Nunny Clo 8 D2

Oak Av 11 E2
Oak Manor Dri 7 E5
Oakfield St 10 A2
Oakhurst Rise 11 F1
Oakland Av 7 E3
Oakland St 11 E2
Oakley Rd 7 F6
Obrien Rd 5 G4
Okus Rd 11 F4
Old Bath Rd 10 D2
Old Gloucester Rd 4 A6
Old Millbrook Ter 6 A5
Old Reddings Clo 8 D4
Old Reddings Rd 8 D4
Old School Mews 11 F3
Old Station Dri 10 C4
Oldbury Rd 5 E6
Oldfield Cres 9 F3
Olio La 12 C6
Orchard Av 5 F6
Orchard Pl 12 B1
Orchard Way 5 F5
Oriel Rd 12 C4
Ormond Pl 12 B3
Orrisdale Ter 12 D6
Osprey Rd 10 B4
Overbrook Dri 7 E3
Overbury St 11 F2
Overton Park Rd 6 B5
Overton Rd 6 A5
Oxford Par 6 D6
Oxford Passage 12 C2
Oxford St 6 D6
Oxford Way 9 G6

Paddocks Clo 6 C2
Painswick Rd 10 B3
Parabola Clo 12 A4
Parabola Rd 12 A4
Paragon Dri 12 C6
Park La 7 F1
Park Mews 10 A3
Park Pl 10 B2
Park St 12 A1
Parkbury Clo 9 G1
Parkland Rd 10 D5
Parkwood Gro 11 E5
Pates Av 9 H1
Patterdale Clo 5 G4
Peacock Clo 8 D1
Peel Clo 11 G3
Pembridge Clo 11 G3
Pembroke Rd 9 E5
Pendil Clo 6 A1
Penharva Clo 5 G6
Pennine Rd 7 F3
Pennsylvania Av 5 F5
Penrith Rd 9 F4
Pentathlon Way 6 B2
Peregrine Rd 10 B4
Pheasant La 8 B2
Piccadilly Way 7 H3
Pickering Clo 10 B3
Pickering Rd 10 B3
Pilford Av 10 D5
Pilford Clo 10 D4
Pilgrove Way 5 E4
Pilley Cres 10 C5
Pilley La 10 C5
Pillford Rd 10 C6
Pine Clo 11 E1
Pinetrees 11 E3
Pitman Rd 9 E2
Pittville Circus 6 D4
Pittville Circus Rd 7 E5
Pittville Cres 6 D4
Pittville Crescent La 6 D4
Pittville Ct 6 D3
Pittville Lawn 6 D4
Pittville Mews 12 D1
Pittville St 12 C3
Polefield Gdns 9 H3
Portland Sq 6 D5
Portland St 12 C2
Porturet Way 11 F3
Post Office La 12 B3
Postlip Way 9 E3
Prestbury Grove Dri 7 G3
Prestbury Rd 7 E4
Prince's Ct 10 A2
Prince's Rd 10 A2
Princes St 7 E6
Princess Elizabeth Way 5 F6
Priors Rd 7 F5
Priory Pl 10 D1
Priory St 6 D6
Priory Ter 6 D6
Priory Walk 6 D6

Promenade 12 B4
Pumphreys Rd 11 F3
Purbeck Way 7 G3
Pyrton Mews 9 E6

Quat Goose La 5 H1
Queen St 6 A4
Queens Circus 12 A5
Queens Ct 9 H3
Queens Par 10 B1
Queens Retreat 6 A5
Queens Road 9 H2

Radnor Rd 9 F5
Randolf Clo 11 E3
Ravensgate Rd 11 F5
Reaburn Clo 11 G3
Red Rower Clo 6 B1
Redding Rd 8 D4
Reddings Pk 8 D4
Redgrove Rd 5 G5
Redthorne Way 9 F6
Redwood Ct 8 D1
Regent Arcade 12 C3
Regent St 12 C3
Regis Clo 11 E4
Richards Rd 6 A3
Richmond Dri 7 E5
Rippledale Clo 9 E4
Rissington Clo 9 F3
Rivelands Rd 5 H2
Rivers Leys 5 F4
Riverside Clo 11 G3
Riverview Way 5 G4
Robert Burns Av 9 E4
Roberts La 7 H3
Rochester Clo 9 H6
Rodney Rd 12 C4
Rolleston Way 9 F4
Roman Hackle Av 6 B2
Roman Hackle Rd 6 B2
Roman Rd 9 G2
Roosevelt Av 11 E1
Rope Walk 12 B1
Rose and Crown
Passage 12 C2
Rosehill St 11 E1
Rowan Way 9 F6
Rowanfield Rd 9 G2
Royal Cres 12 B3
Royal Parade Mews 12 A5
Royal Well La 12 A3
Royal Well Pl 12 A3
Royal Well Rd 12 B4
Runnings Rd 5 G3
Runnymead 9 E6
Rushworth Clo 8 D1
Russel Pl 6 B4
Russel St 6 B4
Russet Rd 5 F5
Rutherford Way 5 G4
Rydal Walk 9 F4
Rye Av 5 E4
Ryeworth Clo 11 G2
Ryeworth Rd 11 F2

Sackville App 6 C3
Sadlers Ct 10 D1
St Albans Clo 9 H6
St Annes Clo 6 D5
St Annes Rd 6 D6
St Annes Ter 6 D5
St Davids Clo 9 G5
St Edwards Walk 11 E2
St Georges Clo 6 A5
St Georges Dri 6 A5
St Georges Pl 12 A3
St Georges Rd 12 A3
St Georges Sq 12 B2
St Georges St 12 B1
St Georges Ter 12 A3
St James Pl 10 B2
St James Sq 12 A3
St James's St 12 D4
St Judes Walk 11 E2
St Lukes Pl 12 C5
St Lukes Rd 12 C5
St Margarets Rd 12 C1
St Margarets Ter 12 C1
St Michaels Rd 9 H6
St Nicholas Dri 6 C2
St Pauls La 6 B4
St Pauls Rd 6 B4
St Pauls St Nth 6 C4
St Pauls St Sth 12 B1
St Peters Clo 5 H5
St Peters Sq 5 H5
St Phillips St 10 B2
St Stephens Clo 10 A2
St Stephens Rd 10 A2
Salamanca 7 G5
Salisbury Av 9 G5
Sandford Mill Rd 10 D2
Sandford Rd 10 C1
Sandford St 12 C5
Sandhurst 11 F3
Sandy La 10 D4
Sandy Lane Rd 11 E4
Sappercombe La 11 F4
Saville Clo 6 D3
Saxon Way 11 E1
School Rd 11 F3

Seacombe Rd 9 E1
Selkirk Clo 6 D4
Selkirk Gdns 6 D4
Selkirk St 6 D5
Selworthy 9 F6
Seneca Way 6 A2
Sevelm 9 F6
Seven Posts All 7 F3
Severn Rd 7 E4
Shakespeare Rd 9 E1
Shaw Green La 7 F1
Sheepscombe Clo 9 E3
Shelburne Rd 9 G4
Shelley Av 9 F2
Shelley Rd 9 E2
Shepards Clo 5 E4
Sherborne Pl 12 D3
Sherbourn 6 D5
Short St 10 B3
Shrublands 11 E4
Shurdington Rd 10 A4
Sidney St 6 D6
Skillicorne Mews 9 H3
Smithwood Gro 11 E5
Smythe Rd 5 H2
Solway Rd 4 D5
Somergate Rd 5 E4
Somerset Av 9 G1
Somerset Passage 12 A3
Somme Rd 7 G4
South View Way 7 G3
Southam Rd 7 G2
Southcourt Dri 10 C4
Southern Rd 10 C5
Southfield App 10 D5
Southfield Clo 10 D5
Southfield Rise 10 D5
Southgate Dri 10 D2
Southwood La 10 B1
Spencer Av 9 F2
Spencer Rd 9 F2
Spring La 7 F1
Springbank Dri 4 D6
Springbank Gro 4 D6
Springbank Rd 4 D6
Springbank Way 5 E5
Springfield Clo 8 C4
Stanley Pl 5 E6
Stanley Rd 7 F6
Stanton Way 9 F3
Stantons Dri 5 H2
Stanway Rd 9 E3
Stanwick Cres 6 A2
Stanwick Dri 6 A2
Stanwick Gdns 6 A3
Station St 12 A2
Stirling Ct 6 A4
Stockton Clo 11 E4
Stoneleigh Clo 10 C6
Stoneville St 6 B4
Strickland Rd 11 E1
Studland Dri 7 G3
Suffolk Par 10 B1
Suffolk Rd 10 B1
Suffolk Sq 12 A6
Suffolk St 10 B2
Summerfield Clo 5 G4
Sun St 6 A4
Sunnyfield La 8 D6
Surrey Av 9 G1
Sussex Av 9 G1
Swallowtail Clo 9 E1
Swanscombe Pl 9 F6
Swanswell Dri 9 F3
Swindon La 6 A1
Swindon Rd 12 B1
Swindon St 6 B4
Sycamore Ct 8 D1
Sydenham Rd Nth 7 E6
Sydenham Rd Sth 7 E6
Sydenham Villas Rd 6 D6

Talbot Rd 9 H3
Tamar Rd 7 E4
Tanners Rd 5 F6
Tatchley La 7 F3
Teme Rd 7 E5
Tennyson Rd 9 F2
Tensing Rd 10 D5
Tewkesbury Rd 4 B1
Thames Rd 7 E4
The Avenue 10 D4
The Bank 7 G2
The Burgage 7 F2
The Close 10 B5
The Gardens 6 D3
The Grove, Cheltenham 7 E6
The Grove, Lansdown 9 H3
The Haver 11 F2
The Hawthornes 9 E5
The Oaks 8 D5
The Park 10 A3
The Redding 8 B5
The Runnings 5 H3
The Strand 12 D4
The Verneys 10 D3
Thirlestaine Rd 10 C2
Thirlmere Rd 9 F4
Thistledown Clo 5 E4
Thomond Clo 6 A2
Thompson Dri 10 B5
Thornbury Clo 9 H1
Thorncliff Dri 9 H3
Thornhaugh Mews 9 E6
Three Sisters La 7 H3
Tilney Rd 6 C2
Timbercombe La 11 F6
Timperley Way 9 E6
Tiverton Clo 4 D6
Tivoli Rd 10 A2
Tivoli St 10 A2
Tom Price Clo 6 D5
Tommy Taylors La 6 B3
Townsend St 6 B4
Trafalgar St 12 B5
Treelands Clo 10 C4
Treelands Dri 10 C4
Trinity La 12 D2
Trinity School La 6 D5
Trowscoed Av 10 C3
Tryes Rd 10 B3
Tudor Lodge Dri 10 B2
Tudor Lodge Rd 10 B2
Turkdean Rd 9 F3
Tylea Clo 8 D4

Ullswater Rd 9 F4
Undercliff Av 10 C6
Undercliff Ter 10 C6
Union St 6 D5
Unwin Clo 8 D4
Unwin Rd 8 D4
Upper Bath St 10 B2
Upper Mill La 7 H2
Upper Norwood St 10 B3
Upper Park St 11 E1
Upperfield Rd 5 H4

Verney Clo 10 D3
Vernon Pl 12 D4
Victoria Pl 6 D5R
Victoria Retreat 10 C2
Victoria St 6 B4
Victoria Ter 7 E6
Village Rd 5 F5
Vineries Clo 10 B5
Vineyard Clo 11 F5
Vittoria Walk 12 B5

Waddon Dri 7 E4
Walnut Clo 6 D3
Warden Hill Rd 9 F5
Wards Rd 9 E5
Warren Clo 9 G5
Warwick Cres 11 F3
Warwick Pl 12 D2
Wasley Rd 9 E2
Water La 11 F3
Waterfield Clo 10 C2
Waterloo St 6 A3
Watermoor Clo 5 E4
Welch Rd 5 F5
Well Pl 6 A6
Well Walk 12 B2
Welland Ct 7 E3
Welland Dri 7 E3
Welland Lodge Rd 7 E3
Wellesley Rd 6 C4
Wellington Passage 12 D3
Wellington Rd 6 C4
Wellington Sq 6 D4
Wellington St 12 C5
Wells Clo 9 G6
Welwyn Mews 9 E6
Wendover Gdns 9 H2
Wentworth Clo 5 E6
Wentworth Rd 5 E6
Wessex Dri 7 F5
West Approach Dri 6 D3
West Down Gdns 6 D5
West Dri 6 C4
Westal Ct 9 H4
Westal Grn 10 A1
Westal Pk 9 H4
Westbourne Dri 7 E5
Westbury Rd 10 C5
Western Rd 6 A5
Westminster Clo 11 E2
Westwood La 7 H4
Whaddon Av 7 E5
Whaddon Rd 7 E4
Wheatland Dri 5 E4
Whitcombe Pl 6 D6
White Cross Sq 10 C2
White Hart St 6 B4
Whitemarsh Clo 5 E4
Whitethorne Dri 7 G4
Whittington Rd 9 E3
Willersey Rd 9 E3
William Gough Clo 5 E4
Willow Rd, Battledown 7 F6
Willow Rd,
Charlton Kings 11 G4
Willowbrook Dri 5 E4
Willowherb Clo 7 G4
Wimbourne Clo 9 E5
Winchcombe St 12 D2
Winchester Way 9 G5
Windermere Clo 9 F4
Windermere Rd 9 F4
Windrush Rd 7 F5
Windsor St 6 D4
Windyridge Gdns 6 B2
Windyridge Rd 6 A2
Winstonian Rd 6 D5
Winterbotham Rd 5 E6
Winton Clo 9 G4
Winton Rd 9 G4
Wistley Rd 11 G5
Withybridge Gdns 4 C1
Withybridge La 4 B4
Withyholt Ct 11 E4
Withyholt Pk 11 E4
Withypool 9 F6
Witley Lodge Clo 9 E5
Wolseley Ter 12 C5
Woodlands Rd 9 H6
Worcester St 6 A3
Wordsworth Av 9 E2
Wychbury Clo 10 B4
Wymans La 6 A2
Wymans Rd 7 E4

Yarnold Ter 5 H5
Yeend Clo 5 F3
Yew Tree Clo 6 B2
York St 6 D5
York Ter 12 A3

GLOUCESTER

Abbey Rd 18 B3
Abbeymead Av 20 A4
Abbotswood Clo 23 F3
Abbotswood Rd 26 B2
Adelaide St 19 E4
Albany St 19 E4
Albermarle Rd 17 G4
Albert St 13 F4
Albion St 18 C3
Alder Clo 15 H5
Alders Grn 15 F4
Alexandra Rd 19 E1
Alfred St 19 F3
Alington Clo 19 F3
All Saints Rd 19 E3
Allendale Clo 15 H5
Alma Pl 18 C4
Alma Ter 18 C4
Almond Clo 24 D2
Alney Ter 14 B6
Alpine Clo 19 G6
Althorp Clo 22 D4
Alvin St 13 E1
Amber Clo 23 E2
Amberley Rd 24 B1
Anbrook Cres 20 B4
Andora Way 16 D3
Ann Hathaway Dri 17 H4
Ansdell Dri 21 G5
Apperley Dri 22 A5
Apple Tree Clo 16 C2
Apple Tree Way 25 E1
Appleton Way 20 D5
Aragon Way 16 C2
Archdeacon Ct 13 B1
Archdeacon St 13 B2
Archibald St 19 E3
Ardmore 23 G3
Argyll Pl 19 G1
Argyll Rd 19 G1
Arlingham Rd 23 F2
Armscroft Court 19 G2
Armscroft Cres 19 G2
Armscroft Gdns 19 G2
Armscroft Pl 19 G2
Armscroft Rd 19 G2
Armscroft Way 19 G2
Arreton Av 19 G5
Arrow Head Clo 24 B2
Arthur St 19 E3
Arundel Clo 23 E5
Ash Gro 25 E3
Ash Grove Clo 22 A6
Ashcroft Clo 24 D3
Ashgrove Av 19 H5
Ashgrove Way 19 H5
Ashleworth Gdns 22 A5
Ashmead 15 G4
Ashmore Rd 23 H1
Ashton Clo 25 E2
Ashville Clo 18 B6
Ashville Rd 18 B6
Askwith Rd 19 G5
Askwood Way 20 C5
Astor Clo 21 F5
Astridge Rd 26 D2
Asylum La 19 F1
Austin Dri 15 E3
Avebury Clo 22 D4
Avening Rd 19 E6
Avon Cres 26 C2
Awdrey Way 23 F3
Awebridge Way 24 C1
Aycote Clo 19 G6

Bader Av 17 E4
Badger Clo 24 D2
Badminton Rd 24 B1
Baker St 18 C3
Balfour Rd 18 C5
Ballinska Mews 16 A4
Bamfurlong La 17 H1
Baneberry Rd 24 A1
Barbican Rd 13 B3
Barbican Way 13 B3
Barley Clo 26 C3
Barleycroft Clo 24 D3
Barn Clo 25 E2
Barnaby Clo 19 E5
Barnacre Dri 20 C2
Barnes Wallis Way 17 E4
Barnett Way 20 B2
Barnwood Av 20 A3
Barnwood By-Pass 20 A2
Barnwood Link Rd 16 B5
Barnwood Rd 19 G1
Barrack Sq 13 B3
Barrington Dri 20 C3
Barrow Clo 22 B6
Barrow Hill 17 F6
Barton St 13 D4
Basil Clo 24 D2
Bateman Clo 23 F4
Bathurst Rd 19 E5
Bazeley Rd 24 B3
Beacon Rd 24 C3
Bearland 13 B3
Beaufort Rd 19 36
Beaumont Rd 15 H4
Bedford St 13 E4
Beech Clo 22 A6
Beechcroft Rd 15 F4
Beechwood Gro 23 G2
Belfry Clo 20 B4
Belgrave Rd 18 D3
Belgrove Ter 19 E4
Bell La 13 D4
Bell Walk 13 C3
Belmont Av 21 E5
Berkeley St 13 C3
Berry Lawn 24 D3
Berryfield Glade 16 D3
Betjeman Clo 23 E1
Bewley Way 16 D3
Bibury Rd 19 E5
Bijou Ct 15 E5
Bilberry Clo 25 F1
Billbrook Rd 20 D4
Billingham Clo 19 G5
Birch Av 19 G5
Birchall Av 24 C3
Birchmore Rd 19 F3
Birchwood Fields 23 G2
Bishopstone Rd 19 F3
Bisley Rd 23 G4
Bittern Av 20 A5
Blaby Clo 25 F1
Black Dog Way 13 E2
Blackberry Clo 25 E1
Blackbird Av 16 A3
Blackfriars 13 C3
Blacksmith La 17 F5
Blackthorne Clo 20 B6
Blackthorne Gdns 22 B4
Blackwater Way 16 A4
Blaisdon Clo 25 E1
Blakeney Clo 23 F2
Blenheim Rd 19 E3
Blinkholme Bridge La 19 G2
Bloomfield Rd 18 C5
Bloomfield Ter 18 C5
Bluebell Mews 20 B6
Bodiam Av 22 D3
Bondend Rd 25 E3
Bourton Rd 23 G4
Boverton Av 21 G6
Boverton Dri 21 G5
Bowly Rd 18 C6
Bradford Rd 19 G1
Bradley Clo 15 G5
Bradshaw Clo 16 B3
Brae Walk 24 D2
Bramble Lawn 24 D3
Bramley Mews 20 D5
Brecon Clo 22 A5
Breinton Way 16 A4
Briar Lawn 24 D3
Briars Clo 16 D3
Bridge Clo 18 A5
Brindle Clo 24 C1
Brionne Way 15 G4
Bristol Rd, Hardwicke 26 B4
Bristol Rd, Quedgeley 22 D2
Brockworth Rd 21 G1
Brook St 18 D4
Brookfield La 17 G2
Brookfield Rd,
Barnwood 20 B4
Brookfield Rd,
Churchdown 17 F5
Brooklands Pk 15 H4
Brookthorpe Clo 23 F3
Brunswick Rd 13 D4
Brunswick Sq 18 D3
Bruton Way 13 E2
Bryerland Rd 26 D2
Buckholt Way 26 B2
Bull La 13 C3
Bullfinch Rd 19 H5
Burleigh Croft 20 C3
Burnet Clo 24 A1
Burns Av 23 E2
Bush Way 16 D4
Buttercup Lawn 24 D3
Buttermilk La 17 E3
Buttington 25 F1
Byard Rd 22 D1
Bybrook Gdns 23 F4
Bybrook Rd 23 F5
Byron Av 23 E2

Calderdale 25 F1
Caledonian Rd 24 C3
Calspick Way 16 A4
Camberley Clo 20 D4
Cambridge St 13 F4
Campbell Clo 16 B2
Campden Rd 23 G3
Campion Clo 24 B1
Capel Rd 24 C3
Carisbrooke Rd 20 D5
Carlton Rd 18 D6
Carmarthen St 19 E4
Carne Pl 19 H2
Carters Orchard 22 B4
Castle Hill Dri 26 C2
Catkin Clo 22 B6
Cavendish Av 17 F4
Cecil Rd 18 C5
Cedar Rd 21 F4
Cedarwood Dri 23 G2
Cellars Rd 26 B3
Cemetery Rd 19 F5
Central Rd 18 D4
Centurian Clo 20 B5
Chaceley Clo 22 A5
Chadwick Clo 23 F3
Chalford Rd 23 G4
Chamwells Av 15 G5
Chamwells Walk 15 G5
Chancel Clo 19 G3
Chandos Dri 26 B2
Chapel Hay Clo 17 F5
Chapel Hay La 17 F5
Charlecote Av 23 E5
Charles St 19 E3
Charlock Clo 24 A1
Charlton Way 15 H4
Chartwell Clo 18 A5
Chatcombe Rd 24 C1
Chatsworth Av 23 E4
Chaucer Clo 23 F1
Chedworth Rd 23 G3
Cheltenham Rd 16 B4
Chequers Rd 19 F4
Cherry Clo 22 A6
Cherry Gdns 20 D3
Cherrywood Gdns 23 G2
Cherston Ct 20 B3
Chervil Clo 24 B1
Cheshire Rd 16 B3
Chesmann Ct 15 E5
Chester Rd 19 H3
Chestnut Clo 22 B6
Chestnut Rd 20 B6
Cheviot Clo 22 A6
Cheyney Clo 19 G5
Chiltern Rd 22 A5
Chosen Dri 16 D4
Chosen Way 20 C3
Church Dri 22 B5
Church La, Barnwood 20 A3
Church La, Hardwicke 26 A4
Church La, Whaddon 23 G5
Church Rd,
Churchdown 17 F5
Church Rd, Longlevens 15 H5
Church Rd, Maisemore 14 A2
Church St 18 C3
Church Way 19 H5
Churchdown La 20 D4
Churchfield Rd 25 E3
Churchill Rd 18 C4
Churchview 20 A3
Cirencester Rd 26 C2
Clapham Ct 13 E1
Clare St 13 B1
Claremont Ct 13 F2
Claremont Rd 13 F2
Clarence St 13 D4
Clarence Walk 13 E3
Claridge Clo 24 D2
Claudians Clo 20 B5
Cleeve Rd 24 C1
Clegram Rd 18 C4
Clement St 19 F4
Clevedon Rd 19 E5
Clifton Rd 18 C4
Clomoney Way 16 A4
Clover Dri, Hardwicke 26 C3
Clover Dri, Hucclecote 20 A6
Clyde Rd 26 B2
Coberley Rd 23 G3
Cochran Clo 17 F4
Cole Av 22 D2
Colebridge Av 15 H6
Colerne Dri 21 E4
Colin Rd 20 A2
Colingbourne Rd 19 F5
College Ct 13 C2
College Grn 13 C2
College St 13 C2
Columbia Clo 13 F1
Colwell Av 20 C2
Commercial Rd 13 B3
Concorde Way 19 G5
Conduit St 19 E4
Coney Hill Par 19 H5